PICASSO

First published in Great Britain
in Gollancz Children's Paperbacks 1994
by Victor Gollancz
A Cassell imprint
Villiers House
41/47 Strand
London WC2N 5JE

Copyright © Aladdin Books Limited 1994
An Aladdin Book
Designed and produced by
Aladdin Books Limited
28 Percy Street
London W1P 9FF

Design: David West Children's Book Design
Researched by Gillian Bainbridge BA Hons, ATC

A catalogue record for this book
is available from the British Library

The moral right of the author has been asserted

ISBN 0 575 05669 X

Special thanks to: Museu Picasso, Barcelona; Giraudon/Bridgeman Art Library; Roger
Vlitos; The Design and Artists Copyright Society for all their help. The publishers
have made every effort to contact all the relevant copyright holders
and apologise for any omissions that may have inadvertently been made.

Printed in Belgium

Famous Children

PICASSO

TONY HART & SUSAN HELLARD

GOLLANCZ CHILDREN'S PAPERBACKS
LONDON

When Pablo Picasso was born, he was so still and quiet that the nurse thought he was dead.

The doctor looked down sadly at the tiny bundle. He took a puff of his long cigar and, with a sigh, blew a cloud of smoke into the baby's face.

Screwing up his face in disgust, Pablo let out a bellow of fury.

"That's more like it!" exclaimed the doctor with relief. The doctor was Pablo's Uncle Salvador. He rushed to tell the good news to the waiting Picasso family - their son and heir had been born.

Pablo Picasso was born in Málaga, southern Spain on 25th October, 1881. Despite the worrying start to his life, Pablo was a strong and healthy baby.

Pablo's grandmother and two aunts lived with the family. They doted on their "Pablito", so little Pablo was used to being the centre of love and attention from his earliest days.

He would sit with his aunts while they embroidered gold braid for railwaymen's caps. Pablo loved the intricate patterns they made.

Pablo's father, Don José, was a painter. He didn't sell much of his work so he took a job at a museum, restoring paintings. Although he wasn't paid a lot, he could use the studio there for his own work.

Don José loved breeding pigeons. Even as a baby, Pablo would often watch his father drawing and painting his favourite subject.

One day Pablo's mother, Doña María, waited excitedly for Don José to come home.

"Pablo said his first word today," she told her husband. "He tried to say "pencil"." Soon he could draw spirals like the snail-shaped fritters he loved to eat.

Pablo's parents were very proud of their son's progress.

"Look, he's not crawling like a baby, he's walking like a man," laughed his father, as Pablo toddled around holding on to a biscuit tin.

On Christmas night, when Pablo was three years old, an earthquake struck Málaga. Don José rushed home to his wife and son.

"We must go somewhere safer," he cried, and throwing on a cape, he snatched up little Pablo and wrapped him in its folds. Doña María pulled a scarf round her head and nervously followed her husband as he dodged through the crumbling streets. Don José led them to the safety of a friend's studio. There, three days later, Doña María gave birth to a daughter, Lola.

"It's time for school, Pablito," urged his mother, when Pablo was five.

"I don't want to go," he cried. "It's damp and gloomy and the teachers are too strict."

Don José carried Pablo, kicking and screaming, to school. But as soon as the lessons started Pablo dashed to the window, hoping to see his uncle who lived opposite, so that he could call out to him to be rescued.

In desperation Pablo's parents sent him to a different school, but still he wasn't happy.

"Why can't I stay at home and draw?" he'd grumble day after day.

"Come and see, Pablo. Here's a new sister for you and Lola," said Don José. "We'll call her Conchita." The baby was beautiful - tiny with blonde hair and Pablo loved her immediately. He was six years old.

Pablo spent hours drawing. He drew pictures for his cousins.

"What do you want me to do?" he asked them.

"A donkey - starting with its back," said María.

"Now one for me, starting with its ear," begged Concha.

Pablo soon borrowed Aunt Eloisa's embroidery scissors to make cut-out pictures of animals, flowers and people.

Age 8

"Do us a portrait of a dog," his cousins demanded and Pablo would do one after another, until he was exhausted.

While the other children played together in the square, Pablo made drawings in the dust. Often he drew the pigeons which perched in the plane trees.

Pablo drew the things he saw around him at home.

"I'll draw "Hercules" from the statue in the corridor," he decided.

He made drawings and paintings of the bullfights he saw. Bullfights were part of Spanish life and Don José loved to watch them. Almost from the time he could walk Pablo would go to the bull ring with his father. A famous bullfighter of that time was El Lagartijo.

Age 9

"I shall take you to see the great picador, El Lagartijo," said Don José. The bullfight was exciting yet terrifying.

"The bull charged the horse twenty times," shouted Pablo.

He remembered that day for the rest of his life.

Age 8

When Pablo was nine years old he took an entrance exam for the secondary school.

"What do you know?" asked the examiner, who was a family friend.

"Nothing," said Pablo sadly.

The examiner gave him some numbers to add, but left the answer on the table.

Pablo saw the answer and remembered it by imagining the numbers were parts of a pigeon!

"The little eye of the pigeon is round like an O..." he thought. He passed the exam.

Pablo was upset when Don José came home with the news that he had a new job and the family must move to Corunna. Pablo didn't want to leave the sun and blue sky in the south for the rain and fog of the north. None of them did.

"I shall miss the busy harbour of Málaga," sighed Pablo as he painted it.

Age 8

To his surprise Pablo loved his new home and was soon running wild.

"Let's play bullfights," he would call to his friends. Jackets would become capes as the boys took turns to be the fierce bull.

At his new school he still filled his books with pigeons, doves, cats and ink blots transformed into people.

Often he was sent to the "calaboose" - a bare cell with a bench - for not concentrating in class. But he always had his sketch pad with him.

"This is not punishment, it's pleasure," he thought.

Don José was now an art teacher and just before his eleventh birthday, Pablo was accepted as a student in his father's class.

Soon he boasted to his father,

"I can draw like Raphael."

He produced his own newspaper to send back to his relations in Málaga.

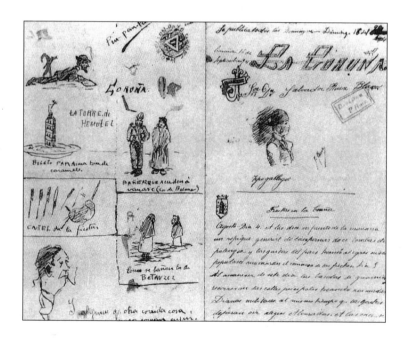

"I am the editor, illustrator, writer and director of my own publication," he announced.

Age 12

At the age of thirteen Pablo became interested in painting portraits.

"I shall make a diary of Lola - getting up, going to bed, helping my mother, doing errands, playing," Pablo decided.

Age 12

Then diphtheria broke out in Corunna and Pablo's beloved younger sister, Conchita, fell ill. The family watched and waited. Pablo prayed. Conchita died at the age of seven and Pablo never got over the sorrow of her death.

Age 12

One evening Don José couldn't finish his painting of a pigeon. He could no longer see clearly enough.

"Can you paint the claws for me, Pablito?" he asked.

When he returned, Don José found that Pablo had painted the claws so beautifully that he handed over his palette, brushes and paint to his son.

"My painting days are over, now," he said.

From then on, Pablo's work improved very quickly.

When Pablo was still only thirteen he decided to exhibit some of his work.

"I shall ask the umbrella shop if I can display my paintings in their window," he thought.

Don Ramón, a local doctor and politician, bought some of the pictures and encouraged Pablo.

Age 13

Age 13

Just weeks after Pablo's exhibition the family moved again. Don José took a teaching job in Barcelona and Pablo enrolled at the art school there. Although the other students were five years older, Pablo soon made friends - especially with Manuel Pallares. Manuel was nineteen and the two of them went everywhere together.

One day they threw a coin on a string from the studio window to the pavement, then made it "disappear" each time someone tried to pick it up.

One very angry gentleman marched up to the studio but when he saw Pablo's painting, he was so impressed that he couldn't say a word!

Pablo Picasso went on surprising people in many ways throughout his life. He married for the first time when he was 80 years old, and died at the age of 92, having become the most famous artist of the twentieth century. He produced thousands of paintings which are now exhibited all over the world.